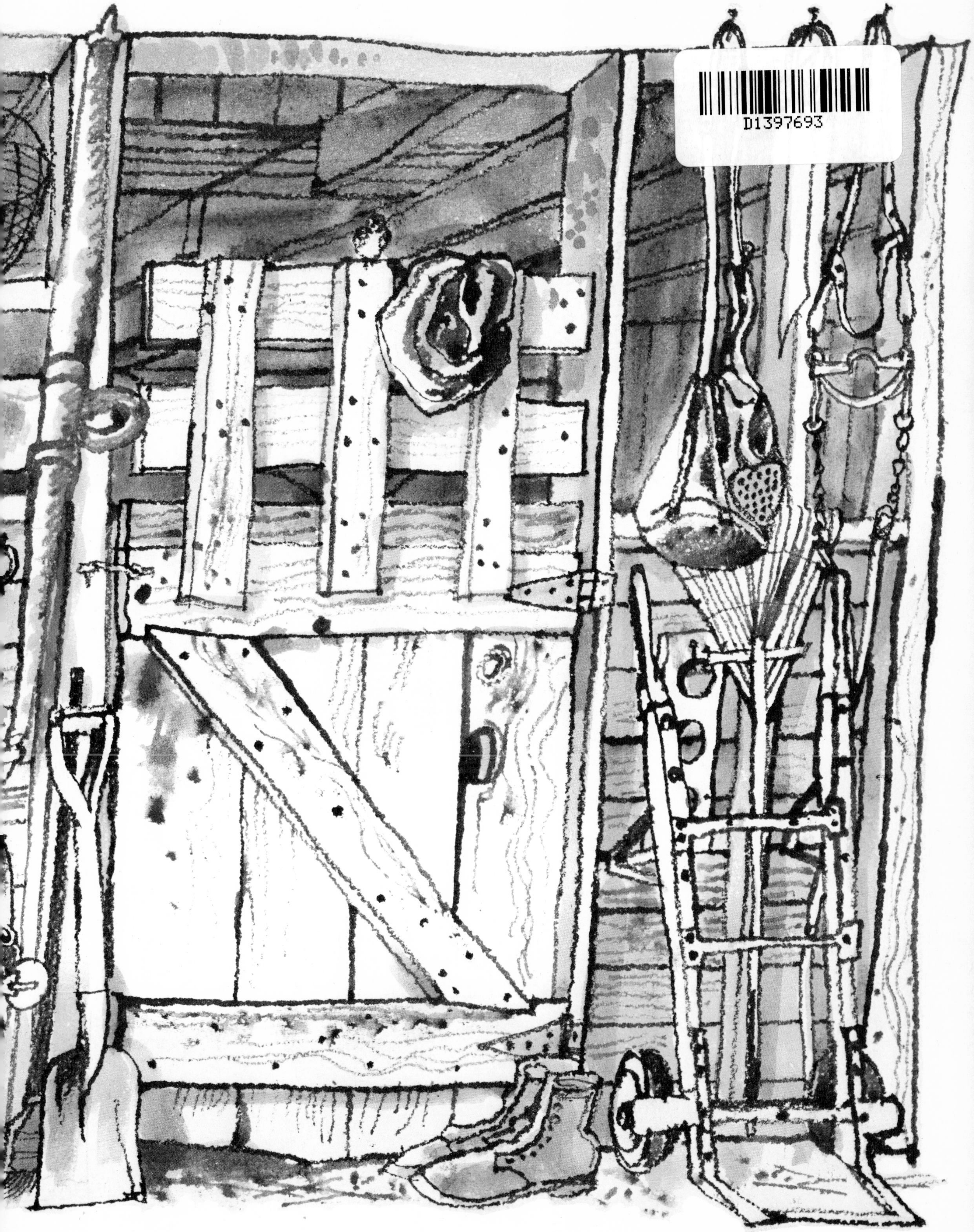

BARNS
OF
CALIFORNIA

This book has been made possible through the generous contributions of:
BELVEDERE SCIENTIFIC FUND, San Francisco
HARRY HILP, San Francisco
PAQUITA LICK MACHRIS, Los Angeles
JAMES F. van LÖBEN SELS, Carmel
and RAY HESTER, Pasadena

Big Nose Barn

Books by Earl Thollander

BARNS OF CALIFORNIA
BACKROADS OF CALIFORNIA
BACKROADS OF NEW ENGLAND

BARNS OF CALIFORNIA

a collection by
Earl Thollander

published by The California
Historical Society

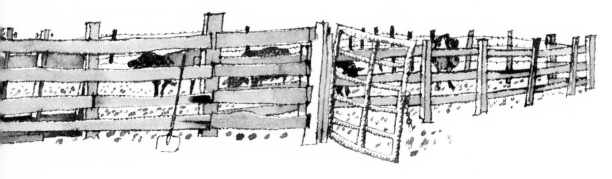

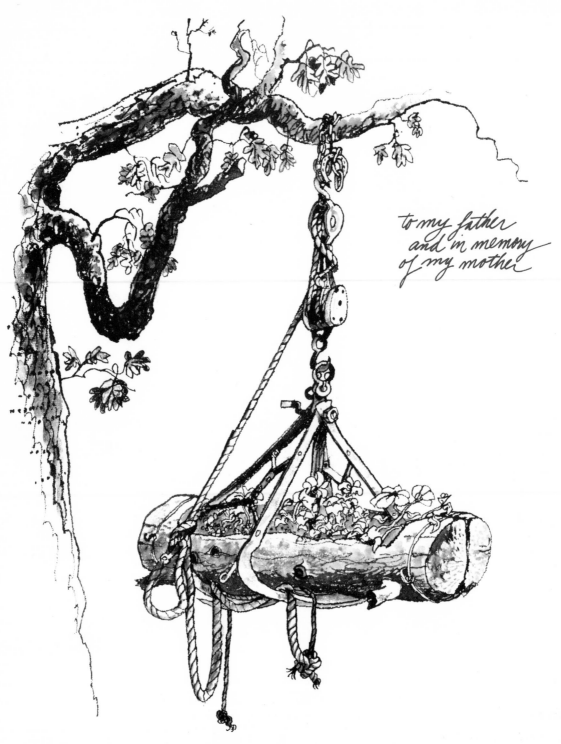

to my father
and in memory
of my mother

Library of Congress Catalog Card Number: 74-78099
Inquiries should be addressed to The California Historical
Society, 2090 Jackson Street, San Francisco, California 94109
First Edition

Preface...

I like barns. There's something good about entering their dark, cavernous, airy interiors and smelling the barn odors. Perhaps you have the same feelings, even though such memories may be vestigial.

Barns once looked right in the farm landscape. Now they seem anachronistic in today's modern agribusiness, a decaying symbol of a way of life that is disappearing rapidly all over America. Many of us, I think, yearn for a return to the more rural living experience. Yet, with more urban population and growth, contact with farm and barn has steadily declined. I'm sorry about that.

From childhood, one doesn't forget the intriguing interior of a barn, with its bigness and its array of hay, farm implements, and animals — chickens, spiders, owls, bats, bees, swallows, and doves.

Barns in California are in every stage of deterioration. The exteriors of some are being sold as fancy wood for interiors. The next windstorm will flatten another. Some are too expensive to keep up or re-roof. Others must be brought down to allow room for crops. Like many historic buildings, however, I feel that barns should be preserved. They are part of the people's history and architectural heritage of our state.

author's note . . .

"You see all that land out there? It's for sale," Mr. Alsford told me resentfully. He was in his late 80's and still vigorously operated the store at San Gregorio in San Mateo County. Formerly this land had been used for grazing cows. Milk and cheese were the products. Now it lies fallow.

What has become apparent to me is the fact that the California barn, as we knew it, has been all but forgotten. Barns were as important as the home itself in the horse-and-buggy days of California. Later they were actively used during the time of the small farmer as hay and feeding barns for cows. Now that farming is done on a grand scale or not at all, apparently the classic barn has become an anachronism—along with the small farmer. Both fell victim to a less personal, faster moving, and more profit-oriented way of life.

Through the courtesy of the California Historical Society, I have been able to search out a representative number of barns and barn-like structures to help memorialize those that still exist. I hope this book will help establish a greater recognition and regard for the esthetic and historical meaning of California barns.

Earl Thollander

Morgan Territory Barn

In 1856, Jeremiah Morgan found the tract of land in Contra Costa County now called Morgan Territory, while he was hunting bear.

Morgan liked the area, so he claimed and fenced the land and moved his family there from Ignacio Valley.

The lumber for the granary on the left, and for the barn, was brought by horse and wagon from the Santa Cruz mountains. Morgan descendents still occupy the land.

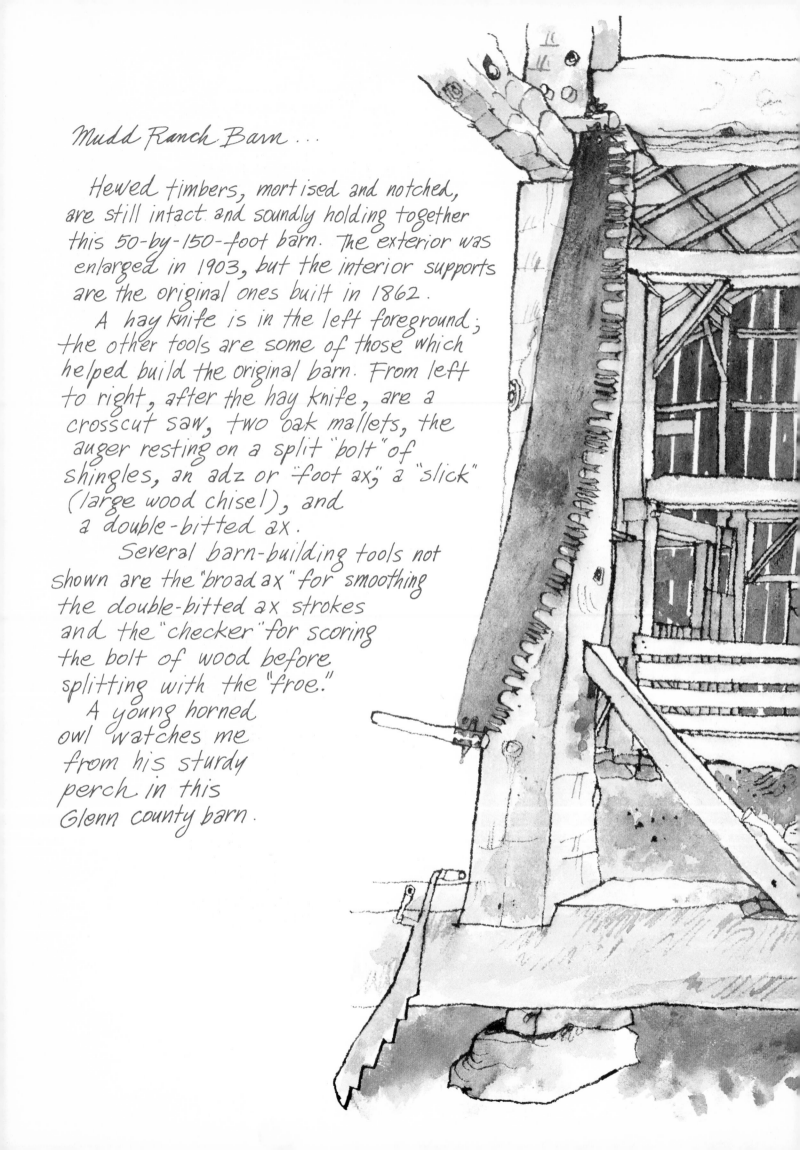

Mudd Ranch Barn...

Hewed timbers, mortised and notched, are still intact and soundly holding together this 50-by-150-foot barn. The exterior was enlarged in 1903, but the interior supports are the original ones built in 1862.

A hay knife is in the left foreground; the other tools are some of those which helped build the original barn. From left to right, after the hay knife, are a crosscut saw, two oak mallets, the auger resting on a split "bolt" of shingles, an adz or "foot ax," a "slick" (large wood chisel), and a double-bitted ax.

Several barn-building tools not shown are the "broad ax" for smoothing the double-bitted ax strokes and the "checker" for scoring the bolt of wood before splitting with the "froe."

A young horned owl watches me from his sturdy perch in this Glenn county barn.

The Strang Barn . . .

Jared Strang came to Sierra Valley in 1858 and
eventually ran five to ten thousand head of cattle
annually. He built his milking barn in 1860 with
hand-hewn timbers.   There is a sketch of it
in Smith and Ferris' HISTORY OF SIERRA, LASSEN &
PLUMAS COUNTIES, published in 1892.

Arthur Strong, grandson of Jared,
still used this barn at the time of my drawing.
He said that the barn is the oldest
in Sierra Valley.
In 1885, the Surrey Barn on the right was
constructed.

LaPorte Road Barn.....

Choosing a definitive "best barn"
of Plumas County to draw
is a frustrating job.
Picturesque barns line the
countryside, sometimes with
four or five side by side.
 I sketched a smaller
barn instead, a barn with
rich pattern, texture and
the warm, natural look of
a structure well-used.

Catholic Mission Barn . . .

The land this barn rests on in Big Valley, Clearlake, California, was purchased by the St. Turibius Catholic Mission in 1867. In 1918, four years after the mission closed, Glenn Keithly bought the property. The original house and church are gone, but the building, the Indian cemetery, and the barn remain. Originally the structure was a carriage and horse barn, then it served cattle and sheep.

Mormon Pole Barn...

The Mormons built many barns in the 4,000-foot-high Genesee Valley along this early stagecoach route between Reno and Sacramento. This Mormon cattle barn is painted bright red and was built in 1852 in Plumas county.
The hip roof on the right is typical, while the roof on the left is a later addition.

Mormon Pole Barn
Interior . . .

Whole logs and poles form
the interior of the Morman
barn. Subsequent owners
have made changes in the
barn, but the essential
pole structure remains.
   As the horse's head
indicates, the old barn
is still in full use.

Wideawake Ranch Barn...

Loose shingles clattered in the wind and this big barn's timbers creaked and swayed. Bats in the rafters added their squeeking. Two large barn owls sat silently overhead and a cotton-tail rabbit loped through. A gutted cat grinned at me from the floor of the barn where he had died.

Emprey and Thomas Hildreth built the 50-stall barn near Merced in 1870. Since it was a stage stop, oxen teams and horses were housed here, often staying a week before going on to Stockton.

The Hildreths named the ranch Wideawake because the meadowlarks sang so melodiously—and so loudly—each morning.

Foss Valley Barn......

There are many rock walls and a long-abandoned stagecoach and post office stop nearby. The broad valley stretches out in front of the barn. Groups of deer graze, and it is surprisingly tranquil for a place so near the modern city of Napa.

Because the land seems not to have changed physically, I can imagine more vividly the stagecoaches and horses housed in this barn 80 or 100 years ago.

Wagonwright's Blacksmith Shop...

Behind the Plaza Stable at San Juan Batista is the long, shed-like Wagonwright's Barn.
   At one time the Butterfield Overland Mail stopped here, and so did the horse-and-wagon traffic between Los Angeles and San Francisco. And in those days, there were plenty of wagons to fix and horses to shoe. The Plaza Stables was built in 1861 and the Wagonwright's Barn soon after.

Clark Foss Barn....

In 1878, a coach and four horses were regularly driven
seven miles from Calistoga northwest over Murray Hill
to "Fossville". The coach was driven by Clark Foss, who
owned the hotel at Fossville, Sonoma County. Visitors could
relax there, eat, refresh themselves, and spend the night
before going on to see the then famous geysers east of
today's town of Geyserville.
  Frank Turner, who lived at the old Fossville site,
has the hotel guest book. It contains the signatures
of many famous people of the day, most notable of
whom was Ulysses S. Grant.
  Today, all that's left is Clark Foss's barn,
creaking and groaning with each wind over its
inventory of farm equipment and paraphernalia. The roof
rafters were alive with bats, and standing inside,
I could hear their scratching and squeeking sounds.

Godward Barn....

Clark Foss would pass this Napa Valley horse barn along the way between Calistoga and Fossville. Square nails were used in the barn's construction over a hundred years ago in about 1872. The stalls are intact and the barn is still used daily for the owner's Black Arabian horses.

Note the dovecote on the side of the barn. Pigeons were often kept for food in barns of the earlier days.

Colorful geraniums grew in the window boxes of this well kept California barn. The window trim is white and the rest is a traditional "barn red".

Howard Joses Whiskey Slide Barn . . . .

The Joses barn may be as old as the nearby
1852 Mt. Ranch Hotel. It is held together
by poles and beams, all under considerable
stress in this Calaveras county barn.
Ankle-biting and tickling flies made me
dance and curse and hurry

to finish my work.
The closer you get to barn
interiors—and the fresher the
cow plops — the more flies you
encounter. I warn you now.

Wickenden Barn . . . .

Fred Wickenden, son-in-law of Benjamin Foxen, built this barn along the former stage route from Santa Barbara to San Francisco.
   In 1880, he drove 5,000 sheep to Redwood City, sold them for a dollar apiece, and spent $2,500 on lumber to build his house. The lumber was shipped to Avila, then horses hauled it the rest of the way. Wickenden had enough redwood left over to build his barn and Sisquoc Church, too, here in Santa Barbara county.

Upper Pierce Point milking Barn...

Old cypress trees and fog give an ominous mood to this coastal farm. The floor beam supports for this Marin County barn were placed on stones. Even so, and after a hundred years, this venerable barn still stands strong against Pacific storms.

The McClures owned this land for some 35 years and milked 300 cows a day in the historic building. Pierce was the pioneer from Maine who bought the land from the Spanish.

Mail Pouch Barn . . .

Eugene Dragovich's father thought he had made a good bargain by letting two sides of his barn be painted in exchange for "Chew Pail Pouch" on the roof.

The painted sign outlived the father. Now it has come shining through a coat of aluminum paint which had obliterated it some years ago. The son and I agreed that it should be left, since such "pop art" of the 30s in Merced county is now of historical interest.

Dragovich Milking Barn...

"It takes 100 to 200 or even 300 milking cows to stay in business these days," said Mr. Dragovich. The cows are lined alongside each other and fed and sprayed with a hose while they are being milked.

Other newer milking barns are circular and cows are in stalls on a merry-go-round. As one cow finishes milking, the stalls turn and another cow takes its place. That way, milking is continuous.

Twin Silos Barn . . .

In the early 1940s, L.B. Hutchison of Indiana added the twin silos, a midwestern touch to his 100-year-old barn. They stand picturesquely in Bachelor Valley. This barn housed the last dairy herd in Lake County, according to the Hutchisons, who sold theirs in 1969.

The Leaning Silos of Sousa . . .

The marvelous wooden silos of
Norman Sousa, with their necklaces
of swallow's nests, lean staunchly in
front of a century old milking barn.
Chopped corn was funneled in
through the door at the top, then
trampled down and watered.
The water allowed for mild
fermentation, and the corn
was fed to appreciative cows.
Today the
herds are gone
from San Mateo county's
San Gregorio Valley, and
the silos have
long since held
their final fermentation.

Butterfly Barn...

This Kings County barn seems to have wings,
which was appropriate for the time I was there.
The alfalfa fields were releasing thousands
of bright yellow butterflies.

Swamp Barn . . . .

Where Swamp barn now stands was originally marsh land. But the Hosselkus family ditched the area and the barn was built in 1921.

It held enough hay to feed 60 cows for five to six months. Sixty calves were born there during March and April of each year.

Sadly, the Plumas county barn is not used anymore, and "will blow down as it weakens," the present owner told me.

Organic Barn. . . .

    Barns are organic to me because the most picturesque
of them seem to be returning to the earth. Barns in
landscape make the scene's beauty even more haunting.
In his need to farm, man's use of the land seems
rational and logical. This was especially true in
earlier times before pesticides and when fertile
land was farmed, not haphazardly covered
with housing and highways. Calaveras county.

Cobb Mountain "Pillow" Barn....

Cobb Mountain barn in Lake County is being pushed to earth. No one seems to care, even though the barn is still in use. The tree blew down some time ago and came to rest with the barn for a pillow. The barn's demise seems certain.

Hughes Bearclaw Barn...

In the 1950s Willard Hughes was losing hogs. When he found out they were being killed by brown bears, he started setting traps. Testifying to his success, a sampling of bear paws is nailed to his Calaveras county barn.

Barns are intriguing to young boys. The big buildings make a good place for a friendly scuffle, and for stuffing your opponent's shirt with hay.   Cats keep having offspring in barns. Eighteen cats and kittens appeared at the door the day I made my drawing.

Fountain Grove Barn interior...

The hayloft of Fountain Grove Barn is my vantage point to draw a portion of the intricate structure of the interior. It is almost abstract. Two octagonal platforms, one above the other, form additional hay storage areas, and doves have an infinite number of roosting places.

Fountain Grove Barn....

Thomas Lake built the Fountain Grove barn with
16 sides in 1873. The stalls, arranged in a
circular pattern, make room for 28 horses.
The barn stands on a hill in full view of
Highway 101 traffic just north of
Santa Rosa in Sonoma County.

Fountain Grove Barn...

Cows came to the molasses tank to lick as
I sketched, or they watched me from the shade
of the barn alcove.
Pigeons cooed.
This is the entrance to the unique
Fountain Grove Barn.

The Round Barn....

This elegant round barn is now the headquarters for the Santa Rosa Corporation Yard, where equipment and parts are stored for the city. The Yard will be moved elsewhere someday. After that, perhaps the barn can become one of Sonoma County's historical sites, and people can visit.

Originally a stable for race horses — according
to one source — or for Wells Fargo stage coaches -
says another source — the barn is in its
hundreth year of service in one capacity
or another. There was a weathervane at
the top of the cupola, but it was
removed because of its deterioration.
Perhaps this too may be restored someday.

Pereira Octagonal Barn...

The octagonal cupola is tilted a bit on this handsomely proportioned San Luis Obispo county barn. To make this drawing, I shared a meadow with a goat, a calf, and a vigorous young bull.

The bull's unrest and periodic charging across the field unnerved me, so I hurried to the drawing's completion. Then I retreated and fled the enclosure with only a slight loss of dignity.

James Lick's Granary Barn...

James Lick's Mill, Agnew, ran four water-powered stones producing 250 barrels of flour a day in 1867. The mill burned down fifteen years later, but the round, brick granary barn is still standing. It is owned by Commercial Solvents Corporation and used for storage here in Santa Clara county.

Kleinsasser Horse Barn . . .

The Kleinsassers, Mennonites from South
Dakota, built this barn in 1913. Jake Kleinsasser
was the principal carpenter; possibly his
design was influenced by the family's
midwest origin. Some say the barn is shaped
like a hat.

John Kleinsasser told me he remembers
hitching up the horse and carraige in this
barn to go visit the girl friend
so long ago here in Tulare county.

Little Lake Valley Barn...

Barns and buzzards grace many a landscape in
California. I've wondered for a long time why
wooden barns, especially old ones, please the
eye so much. Is it because the wood of
the barn relates directly to the trees nearby
and to the earth itself, where the wood
originated? Is it a fact, too, that the
barn shape is a functional and traditional
one, a classic entity that summons
our earliest architctural impressions?
Old California barns don't
scream for attention. They
seem to me to be as
natural as grass.

Spud Howard's Livery Stables ....

    The older folks remember Spud Howard's Livery Stable
in Upper Lake, Lake County. The old hotel is still
standing nearby, and once you could stay there and
rent a livery rig from Spud to get around and do
your business.   Spud did a lot of hay hauling and
delivering in his buckboard for the farmers in the mountains.

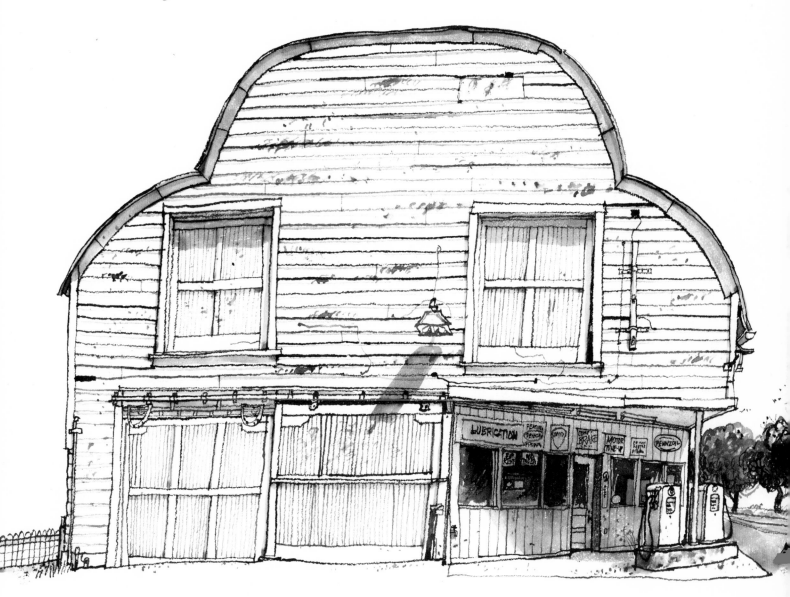

    Here's one way to save an older structure. Slice off a
corner of it, install gas pumps, and use the rest of
the building as a garage. It certainly isn't
beautiful, but the historic structure is at
least preserved a little longer.

Faulkner Barn....

This redwood barn was built in the 1880s. Its timbers were brought by ship to Ventura and then by horse and wagon to the barn site. At one point on the road, the turn was too great for the 50-foot supporting timbers, so they had to be carried past the bend and loaded on the wagons again. The barn was built for $800.

A later Mr. Faulkner was distressed when the barn's value was determined today at $5000. Termites had done such a good job, he told the assessor, that only the spider webs were holding the barn together. Its assessed value was dropped to $200.

Usibelli Barn . . .

   The land rolls a little here in the Napa Valley, and the
Usibelli barn, which you can see from the Oakville Cross
Road is a hundred years old. It gleams white over
the surrounding cool summer green
   of Cabernet Sauvignon vines.

A great red barn of similar design, originally a winery, is close by, and you can see it from Oakville Cross Road, too. Both were put up by the same builder. And both are unusual because they are surrounded by grapevines instead of pasture.

Laufenberg Barn....

The Charles Laufenberg barn in Knight's Valley, Sonoma County, was built in 1883 by race horse fancier Louis McLane. The rich brown redwood siding is still unpainted.

In the 1950s the barn got a corrugated metal roof and so lost its fancy pigeon tower. I agreed when Mr. Laufenberg said "I wish I had that pigeon tower back!" The birds kept returning for years looking for their lost dovecote.

Laufenberg Barn Wall

Barn walls collect all kinds of impedimenta. Among other items, this drawing includes a rat trap, prune dipper,

Bartlett pear grader, hay hook, crosscut saw, and
the following horse trappings: a bridle and reins, halter,
nose bag, neck yoke, singletree, collar and "nose twister."

California Bavarian Barn . . . .

   The Bernard Fords built this Bavarian style barn in 1939.
Tom Williams of Redwood City was the builder, employing
hand-hewn timbers to simulate the old barns of Bavaria.
      Redwood was used, and a coating of linseed oil
   mixed with graphite gives the barn a darkened,
      aged look.
The antlers are attached to a section of redwood
tree trunk serving as a decorative cupola
   for this unique San Mateo county barn.

Lucky Baldwin Coach Barn . . . .

It was a hot, humid August day at the Los Angeles Arboretum.
 I sat sketching Lucky Baldwin's Coach Barn, which is open
  to the public. The peacocks that roam the ground
gave a lengthy and ear-piercing concert.
   The barn is painted a glistening white with bright red
 trim. It's a fancy barn, built in 1879. It housed, then,
   Baldwin's horses and his coach four-in-hand.

Wilder Ranch Horse Barn.....

This elegant stable in Santa Cruz Country was built for horses and carriages; later, polo ponies and rodeo horses put up here.

The stable has blacktop flooring—a forerunner of today's asphalt paving. The petroleum base rock was mined on the Wilder property. It was rolled and melted into place by hand.

Nearby, an 1875 cow barn has mortise and tenon construction and hand-hewn beams.

A cat sat next to me while I drew, and sprinklers rhythmically watered a section of meadow.

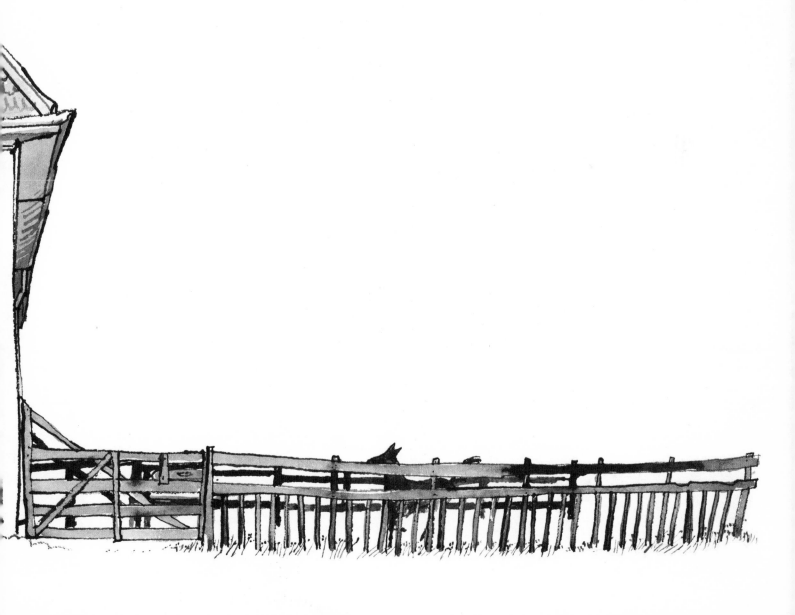

Johnson Coach Barn...

Redlands in San Bernardino County still has some handsome old coach barns. This is one of them, built in about 1887 by a Mr. Johnson. Quarters for the coachman were in the barn too.

The present owner had to do quite a bit of convincing to get someone to risk re-roofing the cupola.

Alsford Window Barn, Sliced Thrice...

    This calf barn is unique, but not just for its many windows. The philosophy of that was... plenty of light makes healthy calves.

    Its other distinction is that in 1948 it was sliced into three sections and moved to get it out of the way of the "new" La Honda road in San Mateo County.

    It is now, obviously, a sheep barn. Cattle and calves are long gone from this part of California.

"Tule" Phillips' Barn...

The King County land hereabouts once belonged to Daniel Rhodes. He and his brother helped organize the first expedition to rescue the Donner party in California's early days. Daniel's daughter Rose married "Tule" Phillips, and he built the barn.

The present owner moved it about two miles to a tree-shaded location and put it on a smooth concrete floor. The interior is certainly interesting with its vaulted and cobwebbed roof, hugh stone fireplace, and hay bales.

The barn has everything needed to entertain a crowd of people for a barbecue, a dance, or for just getting together. The community of Lemoore is fortunate to be able to use the barn for various activities.

JACK'S PLACE
A very respectable dance hall

The Stock Barn...

When Al Stock, carpenter and barn builder, moved from Nebraska to Orangevale, Sacramento County, in 1944, he built this barn. The amount of arch was determined, he told me, by measuring two-thirds the width of the barn, then using this measurement to make the radial curve. Stock bent and nailed together four thicknesses of one-by-four lumber to create the arched rafters. No cross bracing was necessary because the arches, on three-foot centers, gave ample support for the shingled roof. The vaulted interior creates a church-like effect.

Mountain Barn . . . .

This is a Humboldt County barn near Blocksburg.
Its four long sloping roofs give it a tent-like
appearance. Surrounding the barn is a complex
of fencing, which created additional pattern and
texture in the setting. It is interesting that
so many barns retain their originality. Boards are
not replaced, even though they are beaten, scarred,
broken, split, and "woodpecked". This is an
esthetic bonanza for the artist and photographer,
or for anyone interested in how wood ages and
in the historic feel of a place.
Barring the almost universal substitution
of sheet metal roofs for shingles, most
of the old barns remain structurally
intact. They must be one of
California's most authentic architectural
ties with the past.

Olive Oil Factory Barn . . .

Before the horseless carriage arrived in California, horse barns and even mule barns were common. The automobile changed this, and most barns were used for cattle or sheep or just as storage areas for crops and farm equipment.

This barn was probably one of a kind. It became an olive oil factory. It is now a store in St. Helena, Napa County, where you can buy good cheese, salami...

...and olive oil.

Granary Barn . . . .

    The inside-out look, with the exposure of the studs on
the outside, distinguishes the Granary.   The smooth side
is inside for the storage of grains.
    Though it was built to hold feed grains for
raising racing horses, this granary, in Kings County, is
now used for general storage.

Country Grain Elevator "Barn"

This barn-like building, re-constructed by Barret and Hilp in 1952, attains a certain measure of elegance in its skyward thrust. Here on Ryer Island in the delta region of the Sacramento River, safflower, yellow corn, barley and wheat are variously stored.

The M. Theo. Kearney Blacksmith Shop "Barn"...

In the shade of the old walnut tree is the M. Theo. Kearney Blacksmith Shop. It is located to the rear of Kearney Mansion in Kearney Park, Fresno. Olive trees line the street opposite and peacocks pose on the barn roof. They sometimes alarm you with their raucous and "other-worldly" screams.

Martin Theodore Kearney was a wealthy landowner in the 1880s and 90s. Part of his former estate, the loveliest part, is open to the public.

Hop Curing "Barn"...

Gracefully this Sonoma county building leans,
and like old barns everywhere, shows
suspended action wonderfully and
miraculously. Lines tip to the
left and right; none are quite square
or straight. The structure seems
to be earthbound. It may take a
few more years to reach earth,
but you can see the fall coming.
The variety and subtlety of this
action, the patina and patterns of
old wood intrigue the artist.

Harrison Finley Hop Curing "Barn"...

Blue jays rasped and woodpeckers tatted at the Finley Hop Barn roof as I sketched. One roof had completely collapsed. Young weeping oaks and coyote brush grew vigorously in and about the old ruin. The barn was built with some pride around 1890, when Harrison Finley was one of the first men in the area to grow hops. Today, only the stone walls remain.

Dried hops yield "resinous lupuline," which is important in the flavoring of beer. The hop crop was urged along in the drying process by heat generated in the hop kilns. In this Sonoma County barn four tons of green hops could be dried daily.

Cowell Cooperage Barn....

This century-old, barn-like building on rock stilts may look like a hayloft, but it was the Cowell Lime Company's cooperage. The lime kilns are just behind it; the cooked and cooled lime chunks were stored in barrels made in the cooperage. For years hazel wands gathered on the Cowell Ranch were used as barrel hoops. Men were paid a dollar a thousand for gathering them.

The property now belongs to the University of California at Santa Cruz.

McCormick Barn . . .

"It's a piece of furniture," said Mrs. McCormick.
She spoke of the carefully made dovecote on her barn.
The roofs of barns were ideal for raising squab for
the family fare.
      Once the Santa Clara county barn sported a golden
weathervane from President Harrison's summer
retreat at Monmouth, New Jersey.

Benicia Barley Roller and Barn...

   Old barns are often accompanied
by old farm equipment. I would
have enjoyed the sound of a
Benicia Barley Roller in action,
but, as you can see, I'm too late.
The Blacksmith Shop barn
behind is fortunately leaning
away, so the Barley Roller
will not be crushed when the
barn's collapse comes.

The Plow That Stayed In The Barn . . .

This Rube Goldberg contraption, a 1913 Hackney Auto Plow, was purchased new in Tulare County for $2100. It was the first tractor that moved both forward and backward. Only five were sold, and they worked poorly or not at all in most California soils. This Hackney is painted deep red and bright yellow, its original colors.

Jonesville Stagecoach Toll Barn. . . .

Stagecoach and horse barns were common along high mountain roads in the early mining days of California. Here is one still standing in Butte County.

The barn straddled the road in those days and tolls were collected as the miners traveled through.

Barn Work Table...

As the decades rolled by, this barn work table became more and more cluttered until now it serves only as a wide shelf.

Included in this drawing is an elaborate hay hook of the 1880s (to the right of the saws); it resembles an ancient sword. The hook was plunged into the hay bale, then two vicious looking claws were released to grip the hay while it was being lifted.

Also shown is a wire nose bag for a horse, a bee smoker (with bellows attached), and an historic collection of coffee cans.

Bachelor Valley Barn...

The barns in Bachelor Valley, Lake County, are big and beautiful and there are a number to see if you tour the valley perimeter.

THE PEOPLE WHO LIVED THE EARLY HISTORY OF CALIFORNIA WERE, IN THE MAIN, FARMERS. THE BARN WAS THE CENTER OF FARMING ACTIVITY AND FOR THAT VERY REASON ITS IMPORTANCE IN THE LIFE OF CALIFORNIA WAS PROFOUND. ONE FARMER SAID THAT EVEN TODAY HE'D HATE WORSE TO SEE HIS BARN GO THAN TO SEE THE HOUSE GO. "You can build a house anytime," HE SAID, "but a barn like that, they just don't make 'em anymore." THROUGH MY PICTURES I HOPE I CAN BRING BACK YOUR CONCERN FOR THE BARN, BOTH ESTHETICALLY AND HISTORICALLY. AND I HOPE, TOO, THAT OWNERS OF BARNS WILL GIVE THEM ANOTHER LOOK AND SEE TO THEIR PRESERVATION.

McCormack Mower, 1922

Where the barns are....

Essentially, almost all the barns in this book can only be inspected with the owner's permission. Most, however, can be viewed from the roadway, except where I have especially noted their being on more private property.

ALSFORD WINDOW BARN — turn left off Highway 1, eleven miles south of Half Moon Bay, to San Gregorio. The barn is just a little way past Peterson and Alsford Country Store, San Mateo County.

BACHELOR VALLEY BARN — take Highway 20 several miles going west from Upper Lake. Turn north to Witter's Springs and make the loop through the Bachelor Valley, Lake County.

BENICIA BARLEY ROLLER — one mile from Mountain Ranch on Whiskey Slide Road, Calaveras County.

BIG NOSE BARN (title page drawing) — designed and built by Clark Skidmore, located on North Blackstone, Tulare County.

BUTTERFLY BARN — on 13th Avenue, just north of Houston Avenue, a few miles east of Lemoore, Kings County.

CALIFORNIA BAVARIAN BARN — at the end of Bear Gulch Road, two miles from San Gregorio. This is private property, however, and only a request to R.K. Miller by letter would gain permission to see the barn, San Mateo County.

CLARK FOSS BARN — about seven miles northwest of Calistoga in Knight's Valley on Highway 128, Sonoma County.

COBB MOUNTAIN "PILLOW" BARN — what is left of Cobb Mountain Barn is along Bottle Rock Road, about halfway between Cobb and Kelseyville, Lake County.

COUNTRY GRAIN ELEVATOR "BARN"—two miles and a half north of Rio Vista take the ferry to Ryer Island. The grain elevator is along Minor Slough, Solano County.

COWELL COOPERAGE BARN— located at the north end of Bay Street, Santa Cruz, on the University of California at Santa Cruz campus, Santa Cruz County.

DRAGOVICH MILKING BARN— seven and a quarter miles south of Merced off Highway 99, at East Worden Avenue, Merced County.

FAULKNER BARN— near Highway 126 and Briggs Road, two miles west of Santa Paula, Ventura County.

FOSS VALLEY BARN— on a private ranch near the termination of Atlas Peak Road. One must have permission to go through gates, pasture lands, and over dusty roads to reach it; Napa County.

FOUNTAIN GROVE BARN— at 3610 Mendocino Avenue, Santa Rosa. Can be viewed on the right from Highway 101 going north from Santa Rosa, Sonoma County.

GODWARD BARN— about four miles northwest of Calistoga at the head of the Napa Valley, on the left, a quarter mile off Highway 128, Napa County.

GRANARY BARN— about three miles west of Lemoore and Highway 41, Kings County.

HARRISON FINLEY HOP CURING BARN— on the hillside at Ursuline Drive and Mark West Springs Road north of Santa Rosa, Sonoma County.

HOP CURING BARN— on Lytton Station Road off Alexander Valley Road, Sonoma County.

HOWARD JOSES WHISKEY SLIDE BARN— a mile from Mountain Ranch on Whiskey Slide Road, Calaveras County.

HUGHES BEARCLAW BARN — on private property along Jesus (pronounced by natives, "soos") Maria Road, west of Mokulumne Hill, Calaveras County.

Round Valley Barns...

Barns in Round Valley aren't as grand as they used to be. Unhappily, this is also true of most of the other barns in California. The need for barns has declined as the small farmer has been replaced by the corporate farm. There is no longer a living wage in farming small acreage.

I regret the change especially when I see fertile fields and valleys lying fallow, and then often being bought up by housing developers.

JAMES LICK GRANARY BARN—just east of Agnew off Montague Road, Santa Clara County.

JOHNSON COACH BARN— at 709 W. Palm Avenue, Redlands, San Bernardino County.

JONESVILLE STAGECOACH TOLL BARN— go out Highway 32 from Chico to Humboldt Road. Five miles on this road takes you to Butte Meadows. Another five will take you to Jonesville in the Lassen National Forest, Butte County.

KLEINSASSER HORSE BARN— owned by the Downs family, 6365 Avenue 400, Dinuba, Tulare County.

LA PORTE ROAD BARN— a mile along La Porte Road off Highway 70 out of Quincy, Plumas County.

LAUFENBERG BARN— off Spencer Lane in Knight's Valley, about eight miles from Calistoga, Sonoma County.

LEANING SILOS OF SOUSA— two miles from San Gregorio along La Honda Road off on the right a quarter of a mile, San Mateo County.

LITTLE LAKE VALLEY BARN — three-tenths of a mile off Highway 101, west on Reynolds Highway. This is about five miles north of Willits, Mendocino County.

LUCKY BALDWIN COACH BARN— at the Los Angeles State and County Arboretum, 301 N. Baldwin Avenue, Arcadia, Los Angeles County.

M. THEO. KEARNEY BLACKSMITH BARN— located just back of the mansion and servant's quarters in Kearney Park, west of Fresno. Go out Kearney Boulevard through an arcade of grand palm trees and oleanders, Fresno County.

Orange Blossom Road Barn

MAIL POUCH BARN— seven miles south of Merced on Highway 99, at East Worden Avenue, Merced County.

McCORMICK BARN— off Scott Road between Monroe and Cabrillo in Santa Clara. It is on private property, but can be viewed from the schoolyard on Los Padres Boulevard, or from the field at Monroe, Santa Clara County

MORGAN TERRITORY BARN— about seven and a half miles south of Clayton on Morgan Territory Road, Contra Costa County.

MORMON BARN— owned by Mr. Godar in Genesee Valley. It is about three miles beyond Taylorsville and can be seen from the highway, Plumas County.

MOUNTAIN BARN— near Blocksburg on Alderpoint Road going south from Highway 36 at Bridgeville about thirteen miles. Five miles above Blocksburg, Humboldt County.

MUDD RANCH BARN— take Elk Creek Road from Willows west ten miles to Road 302. Go two miles on 302 past the little cemetery to the barn, Glenn County.

ORANGE BLOSSOM ROAD BARN—east of Knight's Ferry, Stanislaus County.

OLIVE OIL FACTORY BARN—in St. Helena go out Charter Oak to McCorkle, Napa County.

ORGANIC BARN—three miles south of the Mokelumne River, six miles south of Jackson on Highway 49, Calaveras County.

PEREIRA OCTAGONAL BARN—about two miles south of San Luis Obispo on South Higuera Street, the old Highway 101, San Luis Obispo County.

THE PLOW THAT STAYED IN THE BARN—in Mooney Grove Museum, Mooney Boulevard, a few miles south of Visalia, Tulare County.

ROUND BARN—located at 819 Donahue Street, Santa Rosa, west of Highway 101 off 8th Street, Sonoma County.

ROUND VALLEY BARNS—from Highway 101 take Highway 261 at Longvale, 30 miles to Round Valley, Mendocino County.

SPUD HOWARD'S LIVERY STABLE—on the main street of Upper Lake, Lake County.

STOCK BARN—between Folsom and Orangevale, at 9060 Greenback Lane. Owned by Al and Kay Stock, Sacramento County.

STRANG BARN—some four miles north of Sierraville on Highway 89, Sierra County.

SWAMP BARN—take Highway 89 to the turnoff for Taylorsville. Go through Taylorsville and ten more miles to Genesee. Chuck Clay will give you directions from Genesee, Plumas County.

"TULE" PHILLIPS' BARN—on private property west of Lemoore and Highway 41 about a mile, Kings County.

TWIN SILOS BARN— about four miles northwest of Upper Lake, off Highway 20. Turn onto Bachelor Valley Road to Witter's Springs. Barn is on the west side of Bachelor Valley Loop Road, Lake County.

UPPER PIERCE POINT MILKING BARN— located just this side of McClure's Beach, Pierce Point Road, Point Reyes National Sea Shore, Marin County.

USIBELLI BARN— turn off Highway 29 at Oakville, Napa Valley. As you approach the Silverado Trail on the other side of the valley, you will see the Red Barn and the Usibelli barn; Napa Valley.

WAGONWRIGHT'S BLACKSMITH SHOP— at San Juan Bautista, a few miles east of Highway 101 and south of Gilroy, San Benito County.

WICKENDEN BARN— southeast of Santa Maria and about five miles southeast of Sisquoc on Foxen Canyon Road, Santa Barbara County.

WIDEAWAKE RANCH BARN— about four miles east of Madera on Highway 145. The road is the next one after the canal and to the left for a mile or so. The barn is owned by Mrs. Vivian Orban Lamon; Madera County.

WILDER RANCH HORSE BARN and other buildings— about one and a half miles north of Santa Cruz on Highway 1, private property; Santa Cruz County.

Epilogue...

Making drawings on location is an adventure. You must be ready to enjoy and marvel at whatever comes along. And you need the nerve and effrontery to sit down and sketch anywhere.

I carry a fold-up seat and look for a shady spot if the sun is hot. I have found, however, that stoic resistance to adversity is often necessary. You must then do yourself proud by submitting, while working, to comfort's limiting conditions offered by flies, ants, bees, gnats, mosquitos, animals, heat glare, cold, cramped positions, wind, flying sand, mud or dirt, children, adults, and, sometimes, the local smell.

My drawing instrument is a stick of bamboo, whittled Japanese style to a blunt, chisel-like point. My ink was Hong Kong's Kwong Yune Kee Ki Company "Writting" Ink. The paper is hand made Millbourne English watercolor paper.

My inspiration for drawing is the works of the Chinese masters and the Japanese masters, especially Seshu and Hiroshige, the books of American Eric Sloane, and the philosophy of Confucious... a picture being worth a thousand words.

EARL
THOLLANDER
Calistoga,
California

Thanks.....to California's historical
societies and Farm Advisors for
helping me find the barns.

Special thanks to Jim Holliday for
believing in this book and
for working so hard and so
long to make it a reality.

Thanks, too, to Paul Johnson for his
help and advice and to
artist Joe Seney for loaning his
camper-vehicle and company
on several long drawing trips.

"Three Sisters", along King Road

This book has been designed and hand-lettered by Earl Thollander in Calistoga, California.
The printing is by offset lithography in two colors by Phelps/Schaefer Litho-Graphics Company.
Jacket design is by John Beyer. Binding is by Filmer Brothers.
The paper is eighty pound Mountie Offset with hand-made finish.